MONEY

KINGFISHER
LONDON & NEW YORK

KINGFISHER
LONDON & NEW YORK

Text and design copyright © Toucan Books Ltd. 2021
Illustrations copyright © Simon Basher 2021
www.basherscience.com

First published 2021 in the United States by Kingfisher
120 Broadway, New York, NY 10271
Kingfisher is an imprint of Macmillan Children's Books, London
All rights reserved.

Author: Dr. Jacob F. Field
Consultants: Dr. Niheer Dasandi; Mert Martens
Editor: Anna Southgate
Designer: Dave Jones
Proofreader: Richard Beatty
Indexer: Marie Lorimer

Dedicated to Jasper and Alienor Niquette

Distributed in the U.S. and Canada by Macmillan,
120 Broadway, New York, NY 10271

Library of Congress Cataloging-in-Publication Data has been applied for.

ISBN: 978-0-7534-7684-0 (Hardcover)
ISBN: 978-0-7534-7685-7 (Paperback)

Kingfisher books are available for special promotions and premiums.
For details contact: Special Markets Department, Macmillan, 120 Broadway,
New York, NY 10271

For more information, please visit www.kingfisherbooks.com

Printed in China
9 8 7 6 5 4 3 2 1
1TR/1220/WKT/RV/128MA

Contents

Money, Money, Money!

Ever since Stone Age people started swapping animal skins for simple tools, humans have been doing deals. Of course, we've come a long way since then. Today, millions of companies trade all sorts of goods with each other all around the world. And their most common resource, available in many different forms, is . . . money!

The world of money involves every business from the smallest local store to the biggest international company, and is full of risks and rewards. It's impossible to survive without money, so it's worth taking the time to understand how things work. Luckily, this book is full of money-savvy characters who can't wait to help you make sense of the stuff. They can fill you in on how to make money, save money, and borrow money — both today and for the future. Come on, let's get started!

Cash

Budget

Bank

Food Costs

Housing Costs

Taxes

Spending Diary

Vacation

Discount

Reuse

Charity

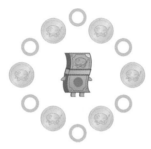

The Money-Savvy Set

Here comes the Money-Savvy Set, a bunch of
characters to help you spend, save, and manage your
money. Who else to lead the gang, but Cash? You'll learn
how to keep track of your money with Budget, and where
to stash it with Bank. After that, it's up to you how you
spend your dough. Check in with Food and Housing Costs,
Tax, Spending Diary, Vacation, and Discount for advice.
And if you want your money to do some good in the
world, resourceful Reuse and generous Charity will
set you on the right track. Now, let's get you in
there so you can meet them all!

Cash
⭐ Big Spender

THE BIG IDEA
Coins and bank notes. You use them to pay for goods (chocolate, for example) and services (a haircut) on the spot.

Bucks, dough, smackers, moola, or cheese — call me what you will, I've been helping people buy and sell goods and services for centuries. I'm Cash, **currency** in physical form, the metal coins and paper bank notes you stuff into your pockets.

I vary from country to country, but my value is always written on my back. As a note, I often feature a fancy device to prevent **counterfeiting** — a hologram, a watermark, or some element that glows under ultraviolet light. Some say I am out of date and that I should make way for super-serious Credit Card and newbie Bitcoin. No way! I'm here to stay!

- The first coins were made in the kingdom of Lydia (now part of Turkey) during the 7th century BCE.

- Through history lots of different things have been used for cash including stones, shells, bricks of tea, beaver fur, bottle caps, and salt.

⚡ SAY WHAT? ⚡

Currency: The system of money that a country uses — for example, dollars ($) and euros (€).

Counterfeit: To make a fake version of an item and try to pass it off as the real deal.

✳ OLD TIMERS ✳

Before people had cash they used a "barter economy." People swapped things with each other — food in exchange for clothing, for example. It was slow going because people had to negotiate the value of the goods with each deal.

Budget
★ Grand Planner

THE BIG IDEA

Plans out how much money a person or company has coming in and how much they will spend over a set period of time.

To get a good grip on your **finances**, have a chat with me, Budget. I can help you keep an eye on the money you have coming in (revenue) and on the money you are spending (expenditure).

Let's say you want to sell cupcakes. First, plan out how much money people will pay for your cupcakes over the next twelve months (your revenue). Then, work out how much it will cost you to make the cupcakes (your expenditure). If your planned revenue is higher than your expenditure, you're onto something and your cupcake business will be a success!

- Governments use budgets to plan how they will pay to run the country. Most revenue comes from taxes.

- A budget should always list essentials first. In a personal budget, for example, basic living costs go at the top of the list: shelter, food, utilities.

SAY WHAT?

Finances: The money that a person or company has at their disposal and the ways in which they use it.

✱ HOW IT WORKS ✱

The most important thing is the "bottom line" — the difference between revenue and expenditure. A higher revenue gives you a "surplus." A higher expenditure gives you a "deficit." If both revenue and expenditure are the same, your budget is "balanced."

Bank
⭐ Deposit Box

THE BIG IDEA

A place to **deposit** money for safe-keeping. Deposited money can earn interest.

You know me — Bank! You'll find me in almost every town and city in the world, standing proud as the most handsome building on the main street (in my opinion).

Visit me in person or use me online, but please keep your money in my vaults. It's much safer than hiding it under your bed. Whenever you need Cash, all you have to do is ask — or head to your nearest **cash machine**. But I do more than store money — see how Credit Card and Loan operate, for example. Plus, I use your deposits to lend money to others. Sure, I charge a fee for this kind of service — how else would I keep myself running?

- The oldest bank still in business is the Banca Monte dei Paschi in Siena, Italy, founded in 1472.

- One of the remotest cash machines is at the McMurdo Station for scientific research in Antarctica. It's 2,000 miles (3,200 km) from the nearest city!

⚡ SAY WHAT? ⚡

Deposit: An amount of cash placed in a bank account.

Cash machine (ATM): A device that allows you to check your bank balance and withdraw or deposit sums of cash.

✳ RISKY BUSINESS ✳

Banks often hold so much money that criminals are tempted to rob them. Very few are successful, however. One of the biggest bank robberies in recent times was in Fortaleza, Brazil, in 2005, where criminals stole $50 million after digging a 256-ft (78-m) tunnel to a position beneath the bank.

Food Costs

★ Money Eater

THE BIG IDEA

Money spent on products that humans eat either raw or cooked in order to grow, stay healthy, and survive.

I'm Food Costs, possibly the most important thing on Budget's list. I'm guessing you don't grow foodstuffs yourself, in which case you'll need a ready supply of Cash to get them to your plate. That's where I come in. My rates partly depend on the **supply chain** — how far food has to travel to get to your kitchen, for example, and what happens to it on the way.

In the past food was grown locally. These days, it has a more international flavor and is more varied, too. It means you can take your pick of exotic fruit and veggies and try native dishes from places you've never been to. But that can set you back!

- The world's oldest recipe was found on a stone tablet in modern-day Iraq. Around 4,000 years old, it gives instructions for making lamb stew.

- The costliest ingredient by weight is the spice saffron. Just 1lb (450g) of saffron can cost over $5,000.

⚡ **SAY WHAT?** ⚡

Supply chain: The system of different people and businesses that take food, or other goods, from where they are produced to the customer.

✳ **HOW IT WORKS** ✳

A huge amount of the food we eat passes through a food-processing facility of one kind or another. This is a place where raw materials are turned into ingredients or products — for example, where grain gets ground into flour for making bread, cakes, and cookies.

Housing Costs
⭐ Home Helper

THE BIG IDEA

Money paid out for accommodation, including rent, household bills (for electricity, telephone, Internet), and local taxes.

See the water running into your bath, the rug you spilled your milkshake on, and the electricity that powers your night light? All of these things (and many more) come under my umbrella. I'm Housing Costs.

For most people, the largest expense is the home itself. Some people rent, while others own their homes, paying regular sums of money toward them. My pal Mortgage will explain how that works. Then there are day-to-day maintenance and cleaning bills. I also account for **utilities**, home insurance, and taxes paid to local governments for things such as garbage collection. Get Budget to put me first and I'll keep that roof over your head.

- Hong Kong has the highest housing costs in the world; monthly rent for a one-bedroom apartment is $2,300.

- In Bulgaria a one-bedroom apartment costs closer to $260 a month.

⚡ **SAY WHAT?** ⚡

Utilities: Services used by everyone, such as electricity, gas, water, sewage, and Internet. Utilities are often run by private companies or, sometimes, by the government.

✳ STRANGE BUT TRUE ✳

In Britain during the 18th and 19th centuries, people paid a window tax. The more windows their houses had, the more tax they paid. Some people bricked up windows in their houses in order to save money. You can still see these in some of London's older buildings today.

Tax

★ Fund Generator

THE BIG IDEA

A charge paid to the government, largely to help fund public services such as hospitals, police, the military, and schools.

OK, OK, I know I'm unpopular, but please know that you have me to thank for your free education and household garbage collections. I'm Tax, a charge people pay to the government, which the government then uses to help pay for public services.

"Direct taxation" is a charge on **income**. It's paid straight to the government and is used to fund such things as transport, health care, and the military. "Indirect taxation" is a charge on goods and services (a computer, say). Called sales tax, the charge is a percentage of the total price. The buyer or user pays it and the seller passes it on to the government.

- Ancient Egypt's government was the first to collect taxes, in 3000 BCE.

- In 1698 Russian Tsar Peter the Great taxed men with beards! He wanted to adopt Western European fashions and hoped his subjects would shave off their beards to avoid the tax.

SAY WHAT?

Income: Money earned on a regular basis, such as wages from a job or a payout from some kind of investment — rent from a property, for example.

✳ HOW IT WORKS ✳

While a national government runs an entire country, local governments operate in smaller areas such as towns, cities, counties, or states. They run and maintain community services such as sewers, roads, public transport, and fire services.

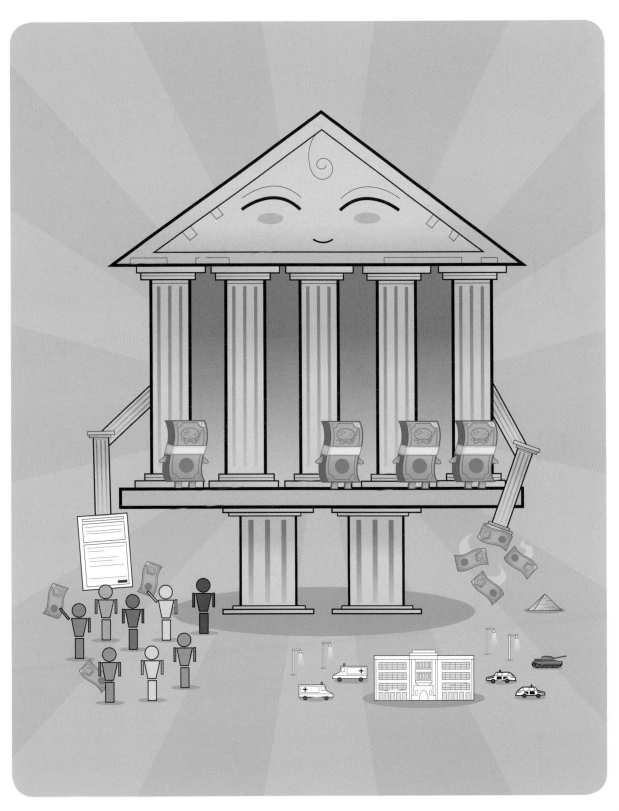

Spending Diary
⭐ Transaction Tracker

Do you struggle to keep track of your spending? Ever think your pocket money runs out too quickly? I'm Spending Diary, and I'm here to help.

Whenever you make a **transaction**, use me to record all the details — when, where, what, why, and how much! Be straight with yourself and do this every time you spend money, whether that's in a shop or online. Understand your spending patterns and you'll spend your money more wisely. Instead of blowing precious Cash on small treats, you could save up for something you really want. Come on, get a grip!

- You can keep a spending diary using an app on your smartphone.

- If you are just itching to spend some money it is said to be "burning a hole in your pocket."

SAY WHAT?

Transaction: Any instance in which goods or services are bought or sold, usually for money. Transactions can be made face-to-face, by phone or online, using cash or a credit card.

✳ DO IT YOURSELF ✳

Keep a spending diary for three months. Add up what you spend each week, and plot the amounts on a graph that you pin to your bedroom wall. See if having a visual record of your spending encourages you to save money. Decorate your graph with a picture of the thing you're saving for.

Vacation

★ Break Taker

THE BIG IDEA

A planned break from work or school. Many employees get a set number of days of paid vacation per year.

School's out for summer! I'm Vacation. Who doesn't love time off now and again? Come and join me on a well-earned break.

It's time to have fun! You can spend days out with friends, go visit that long-lost cousin, travel abroad to see new places, or just do *nothing*! Some adults even get paid when they are away from work. I know! Their employment **contracts** include a specified number of days of "paid leave" — time off while still receiving a wage. Well, what are you waiting for? Get those bags packed, and let's go!

- Companies in Kuwait offer 35 paid vacation days per year, minimum.

- The world's most expensive hotel room is the Empathy Suite at the Palms Casino Resort, Las Vegas. It costs $100,000 a night!

SAY WHAT?

Contract: A legal agreement that sets out the details of a business arrangement (including pay) — for example, between a company and their employee.

THE SMALL PRINT

An employee should always check a contract closely. Some companies expect workers to telecommute while on vacation. That is, they ask them to work for some of their time away, either online or over the telephone.

Discount

★ BOGO King

THE BIG IDEA

When a manufacturer or retailer offers goods or services at reduced prices to encourage higher or faster sales.

Got your eye on a bike, but don't have enough money to buy it? Come and find me — Discount! I'll get you a great deal!

I hang out in stores, reducing the prices of things on sale. **Retailers** use me to free up space on their shelves or to sell off fresh foods approaching their sell-by dates. Sometimes I take the form of a coupon printed in a newspaper or magazine, perhaps offering a BOGO deal (buy one get one free. Geddit?). **Wholesalers** make good use of me too, when they have an especially large number of an item to sell or want to promote a new product — a book or a game, for example.

- Coca-Cola introduced the first-ever sales coupon in 1887.

- A discount store specializing in one type of product — for example books or furniture — is called a category killer. Rival stores that cannot compete with their low prices fail to survive.

SAY WHAT?

Retailer: A seller of goods or services to customers (for example, a shopkeeper).

Wholesaler: A seller of manufactured goods or fresh produce to retailers.

HOW IT WORKS

Specific groups can benefit from discounts in stores, museums, and cinemas. Fortunately for you, children and students are one of those groups. So are retirees, teachers, military personnel, and medical staff. Next time you buy something, check to see if you can get some money off!

Reuse

★ Life Extender

THE BIG IDEA

Extending the life of a product, either by finding a new user for it or giving it a new purpose entirely.

Wow! You humans can be so wasteful! Please, pair up with me, Reuse. Not only will you save money by buying fewer things, but you'll help the environment, too.

At your next birthday party, don't throw away the wrapping paper, boxes, and ribbons. Save them to reuse on presents you give to others. And when you grow out of your shoes, pass them on to someone with smaller feet. That way, they save money, too. Best of all, reusing stuff means less trash ends up as **landfill** and fewer items get made in the first place. These are both massive pluses when it comes to cutting down on **pollution**.

 Paraguay, in South America, has a kids' orchestra that plays instruments made of things reused from landfill.

Trucks delivering to 85 McDonald's restaurants in India are trialing the use of biofuel made from discarded cooking oil.

SAY WHAT?

Landfill: A big hole dug into the ground and used for storing waste.

Pollution: Harmful substances that enter the natural environment — for example, during the manufacture of goods.

HOW IT WORKS

Recycling helps to save both money and the environment. When something is recycled it is broken down into raw materials that can be used again. For example, a glass bottle can be cleaned, crushed, melted, and reshaped to make something new.

Charity

★ Great Donator

> ### THE BIG IDEA
>
> The act of giving to people in need or supporting causes that can help them without expecting anything in return.

I'm Charity, the ultimate do-gooder! Get to know me and you'll see how you, too, can make the world a better place.

Maybe you want to help people who don't have enough food to eat or clothes to wear. Or perhaps you'd like to support research into new medicines. It's hard to make a difference on your own, but make a donation to me and I'll see it reaches the right people. To encourage others to give money, governments often make donations **tax deductible**, and you can give books, clothes, food, anything. Believe me, things you take for granted are often missing in the lives of others.

- In 2016 France became the first country to ban supermarkets from throwing away unsold food, requiring them to donate it to charity instead.

- School groups in the United States raise more than $1.5 billion every year selling various products.

⚡ SAY WHAT? ⚡

Tax deductible: Where money earned is not taxed. If you earned $50,000 a year but gave $5,000 to charity; the government would only tax you on $45,000.

✳ MONEY HEROES ✳

People who spend time and money promoting good causes are called philanthropists. Perhaps some of the most active in the world are Bill and Melinda Gates. In 2000 they started a foundation aimed at improving health care and education and reducing world poverty.

Business

Wages

Interest

Investment

Stock

Bond

Gold

Currency Trading

Bitcoin

The Money Makers

Make way for the Money Makers, the cash-rich characters who can tell you how to make your money grow. First, meet Business to find out how true money makers operate. Then, let Wages and Interest explain how people earn and borrow money. After that, there's no end to the different ways in which you can grow your savings. Money-making buddies Investment, Stock, Bond, Gold, Currency Trading, and Bitcoin reveal all.

Business
Busy Body

THE BIG IDEA

Organization that brings goods and services to the public, with the aim of making money.

What do the following have in common: a supermarket, a gym, an online music-streaming service? That's right! They're all types of me, Business! I'm just crazy about buying and selling stuff — anything and everything from ice cream to computer games and apple pies to apps.

Sometimes I have just one owner, who is responsible for everything (although they may hire people to work for them). I can also be a partnership or a corporation, where two or more people make the decisions. No matter what shape I take, my main goal is to make a **profit**. Busy, busy, busy, that's me!

- A survey in the United States showed that Tuesday was the most productive day of the week.

- Walt Disney World has sold more than 80 million "mouse ears" to date.

SAY WHAT?

Profit: The money a business has left over once all of its costs have been paid (for example, on materials or staff).

STRANGE BUT TRUE

Some businesses do not seek to make money. So-called "nonprofit" organizations perform charitable activities — for example, for scientific research or promoting education. Any money left after paying costs goes straight back into the cause.

Wages
⭐ The Paymaster

THE BIG IDEA
Money that is paid to people in exchange for carrying out work on behalf of a person, business, or company.

Hands up if you think pay day is the best day! Sure, everyone loves me, Wages! I'm what people get in return for all that time they spend hard at work.

Most people know me as their salary. This is an agreed amount that is paid daily, weekly, or monthly. But some people earn a **fee** each time they complete a certain task (for example, making a funky hat or babysitting a neighbor's kids). If they do an especially good job or meet a set target, an **employee** might even get a bonus. And, then, gracious me, there's the tip (also known as a gratuity) that a worker might get from a customer.

- Soccer player Lionel Messi has the highest salary of any athlete in the world, earning more than $90 million a year at FC Barcelona.

- Many countries in the world have a minimum wage. This is the lowest amount of money that people can legally be paid per hour.

SAY WHAT?

Fee: A fixed sum of money that is paid or charged for a service.

Employee: Any person who is paid wages when working for an organization (referred to as their employer).

STRANGE BUT TRUE

In 1984 a New York policeman named Robert Cunningham offered to split the winnings of his lottery ticket with his waitress Phyllis Penzo instead of leaving a cash tip. When he won, they each got $3 million!

Interest

⭐ Borrower's Fee

THE BIG IDEA

A person or organization that borrows money must pay a fee (interest) to whomever they borrowed it from (the lender).

Money always comes at a price, I say. I'm Interest, a tidy sum paid by someone who borrows money. I make sure that the lender receives a payment in return. Hey, nothing's free in my world!

Say you want a new tablet, but it will take ages to save up for it. Your aunt can lend you the money to buy the tablet today, on condition that you pay her back in full a little at a time. Yay! But watch out! Your aunt is a true money-maker, and wants to add me to the mix. Now, not only do you have to repay the **principal**, but also a **percentage** of the amount you borrowed in the first place (that's me). Ouch!

- Keep your money in a bank and the bank may pay you interest on the funds you deposit!

- It may seem a long way off, but if you plan to go to college and need a student loan, you will have to pay interest on the money you borrow.

Investment

⭐ Big Thinker

THE BIG IDEA

When money is spent on an item that is expected to be worth more when sold at a later date (for example, a house).

Let me help you plan for your financial future. Sure, deposit your money with Bank and, yes, Interest will make you a little richer. But, come on! Think BIG, and use me, Investment, to get a *real* **return**.

That's right, choose me, and I'll pay back your original sum, plus a healthy profit. You can do this by buying a property to rent out or by working with my pals Bond and Stock. You'll need patience, though, as I usually only bring results after years, even decades! Oh, and there is one teeny-tiny catch . . . investments don't always work out. Some never pay out at all, and others even lose money. No pain, no gain, I say!

- Asa Candler bought the Coca-Cola Company for $2,300 in 1891, and sold it for $25 million 32 years later.

- The hugely successful investor Warren Buffet began building his investment **portfolio** at the age of 11, buying just three shares in a gas company.

Stock

⭐ Shareholder

THE BIG IDEA

Buying stock is a way of investing in a company by owning a small part of it, known as a "share."

Are you game for a money-making rollercoaster ride? Then get on board with me. My name is Stock. I am one part of a whole company, and you can buy me! You see, some companies are divided into **shares**, which are then sold to the public. Buy some of those shares, and you'll have me, Stock. As a shareholder, you'll own part of the company and might receive a **dividend** each year. You might even get to have a say in how the company is run.

And the rollercoaster? Well, if a company does well, my value goes up, up, up, and you make money. But if things go badly, my value goes down, down, down . . .

- On October 9, 2018, the company Berkshire Hathaway's stock reached $335,900 per share. A record high!

- In 2005 a Japanese bank mis-sold 610,000 shares in a company for 1 yen each (less than a penny), instead of one share for 610,000 yen. Ooops!

⚡ SAY WHAT? ⚡

Share: One of the equal parts into which ownership of a company is divided.

Dividend: A payment that a company makes to its shareholders.

✳ OLD TIMERS ✳

The first company to offer its stock for sale to the public was the Dutch East India Company in 1602. It was founded to trade things like silk and spices in and with Asia. The company continued to trade until 1799.

Bond

⭐ Long-Term Lender

THE BIG IDEA

A way for an organization to borrow large sums of money from lenders.

My name's Bond . . . no, not James Bond! I help companies, cities, and countries raise money to pay for big projects (mega stadiums) or improvements (road repairs). Like 007, I'm strong, solid, and dependable.

Check out my maturity date! That's the date when an organization needs to pay back my value to the person who holds me. It can be years in the future or even **perpetual**. Then there's my coupon. This states how much interest should be paid to the bondholder, usually annually, until I mature. True to my word (and way more reliable than Stock's ups and downs), I almost always guarantee bondholders a regular payment over a long term.

- Bonds used to be issued on paper, with a coupon attached for each interest payment.

- When an interest payment was due, the bondholder detached a coupon in order to receive payment.

SAY WHAT?

Perpetual bond: A bond that has no maturity date. The organization that issues the bond pays interest forever.

HOW IT WORKS

Each bond represents a proportion of the total amount an organization wants to borrow. For example, if a tech company needs to raise $10 million to develop a new type of drone it might issue 10,000 bonds, each worth $1,000.

Gold
⭐ Precious Metal

THE BIG IDEA

The most valuable of the rare metals known as "precious."

What's bright, yellow, and loved by all (besides rubber ducks and the tears-of-joy emoji)? Ha! It's me, Gold! Treasured since ancient times, I'm rare and easy to shape into bling things such as medals and jewelry. Once upon a time I was also the go-to metal for making valuable coins.

Along with other precious metals (I'm talking silver and platinum), big thinker Investment just loves me! Sure, my value goes up and down, but I will always be in demand. So, it's never a bad idea to buy some **bullion** — aim high and choose me!

- Around 209,408 tons (190,040 tonnes) of gold have been mined throughout history — enough to make a cube measuring about 70 ft (21 m) each side.

- The most valuable coin in the world is Australia's Kangaroo One Tonne Gold Coin. It's worth more than $60 million Australian dollars ($43 million).

Currency Trading
⭐ Foreign Exchanger

THE BIG IDEA

Swapping the currency of one country for that of another. It can be done as a form of investment or for spending overseas.

I'm Currency Trading — your travel-friendly pal! Almost every country has a currency for buying goods and services. The UK has the pound, the US has dollars, and the **Eurozone** has the euro, for example.

Say you travel abroad and want to buy an Eiffel Tower fridge magnet, an "I heart Tokyo" T-shirt, or a pair of Turkish slippers (all essential souvenirs, right?). To do this you'll need the right currency and that's when you should call on me. I just use a foreign exchange dealer to get you what you need. (They charge a fee for this service, but what can you do?) **Exchange rates** yo-yo up and down depending on demand.

- There are at least 180 currencies in the world.

- Each country's currency has a three-letter alphabetic code. For example, the Canadian dollar's is CAD.

SAY WHAT?

Eurozone: 19 countries that chose to have the euro as their currency. They are all members of the European Union.

Exchange rate: The value of one currency when converted to another.

STRANGE BUT TRUE

The US dollar is the world's most traded currency. It features in more than eight out of every ten currency trades. People, companies, and countries hold on to US dollars because they know they will always be valued — more than two-thirds of all US dollars are outside of the US!

Bitcoin
★ Digital Money

THE BIG IDEA

A currency that only exists digitally — it has no banknotes or coins. It is used to purchase things online.

Cash? Who needs that *spent* force with me around?! I'm Bitcoin. Hitting the scene in 2009, I may be the baby of the Money Makers crew, but I am the future.

I'm a **cryptocurrency** — a unique piece of computer code stored in a virtual wallet. My spender needs a password to access me. Each transaction is recorded using something called a **blockchain**, which stops me getting spent more than once. People called "miners" use powerful computers to keep track of my activity. And even though anyone can see when I've been used, my spender remains totally anonymous.

- Bitcoin can be purchased using traditional currencies.

- There are more than 5,000 cryptocurrencies. They include Ethereum, Ripple, Litecoin, and Tether.

⚡ SAY WHAT? ⚡

Cryptocurrency: A digital currency that is not controlled by any government or bank.

Blockchain: An online record of transactions that is stored across millions of computers.

✳ THE SMALL PRINT ✳

Investing in Bitcoin is risky. Since it is not controlled by a government, it is very difficult to get back if it is lost or stolen. Some governments want to limit or control cryptocurrencies because they are sometimes used to buy illegal goods online.

Capital

Company

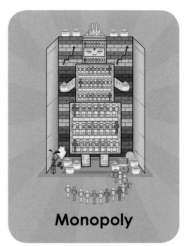

Monopoly

Recession

Depression

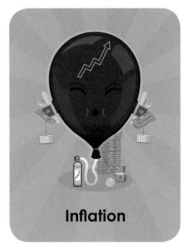

Inflation

Globalization

The Economists

They're in the news every day of the year and there's no escaping them — they are the Economists! These movers and shakers will fill you in on the ups and downs of the financial world. Leading the team is Capital, the source of wealth, followed by Company, which is how many businesses are organized. Prepare to meet a (mostly) bad-rep quartet — Monopoly, Recession, Depression, and Inflation — before getting to know Globalization, one of the most powerful forces in the modern world.

Capital
★ Start-Up Pal

THE BIG IDEA

Another word for financial wealth; the money or **assets** that enable a business to start up and keep running.

Capital with a big "C," that's me, and I mean business . . . no, really! Remember cake-maker Budget? Sure, go ahead and calculate this and that, but you won't get a penny until the cakes are baked, right? So, who's buying the ingredients? I am! I'm the money you need up front to get started — the "readies," as Cash might say.

I'm also anything you use to run your business (think food mixer, oven, cake stall). I'm also any asset you use to expand your business — you've met Money Makers Investment, Stock, Bond, and Gold. Plus, I'm just like a set of building blocks. The greater your profit, the higher I go!

- One way to raise capital is to collect payment first and use that to make the goods.

- The owner of Shutterstock, an online photo library, hired out his own 30,000 images to raise capital; the library now has 200 million images.

SAY WHAT?

Asset: A resource that is owned by a business or individual, and that they can sell to convert into money if needed.

✳ DO IT YOURSELF ✳

Another type of capital is "human capital." This is the experience, knowledge, skills, and habits an individual has that help them to do things like grow the value of a company or develop new ways of doing things. You're growing your own human capital just by reading this book!

Company
★ Firm Friend

THE BIG IDEA

Any organization that runs a business.

Want to get down to business? Then come and have a chat with me: I'm Company, a group of people that run a business together. In fact, I could amount to just one person . . . or thousands. I can be public or private. I might be a partnership, a corporation, or an association.

Say you and your friends want to develop a fun face-filter app — say chee–eese! Just register me with the government, and I will sign contracts, hire workers, borrow money, and pay taxes for you. Better hope you do a good job, though. If you don't, I could get *liquidated*. Yikes!

- Founded in 578 CE, the oldest company still running today is Kong Gumi, a temple builder in Japan.

- A private company has a small number of owners.

- A public company is all or partly owned by people who buy shares.

Monopoly
★ Market Dominator

THE BIG IDEA

When an organization has complete control over a product or service within a given area.

I'm Monopoly — no, not the board game! Believe me, I don't play around in my pursuit of **market dominance**. Mwahaha! My goal is to be the only organization that sells or provides a certain product or service.

My plan is simple. First, I make it difficult for rival companies to gain customers. Then, with those losers out of business, I can raise my prices as high as I like. Ha! I'm illegal in some countries, but I wear many disguises. For example, you could say that Google has a monopoly over Internet searching in many countries because it's too big and successful to compete against. Just you try taking them on!

- In the board game Monopoly players aim to force opponents into bankruptcy by buying and developing properties.

- Steel, diamonds, coal, petroleum, and salt are all natural resources that have been monopolized.

⚡ **SAY WHAT?** ⚡

Market dominance: When just one organization controls most of the sale of a particular good or service in an area.

✳ **THE SMALL PRINT** ✳

There are devious ways to achieve a monopoly — as a cartel, for example. This is when a number of organizations work together (often in secret) to dominate the market as a group. By selling things cheaply, they can drive competitors out of business. Then they can raise their own prices.

Recession
★ Downturn Woe

> **THE BIG IDEA**
>
> A decrease in business activity in a particular place, lasting for at least a few months.

Look, I know I have a bad rep, but all I'm saying is you can't have a boom without a bust. And I'm Recession, a.k.a. the "bust."

A natural part of the business cycle, I follow a period of economic growth (the "boom"). I hang around for at least a few months or even a couple of years. People lose their jobs when I'm around. Companies go out of business and **GDP** stops growing. But it's not all my fault! Sometimes people lose confidence and just stop spending. Or something like an earthquake or outbreak of disease stops business activity for a while. I'm never permanent, and recovery is usually just around the corner.

- There is at least one global recession every decade — a worldwide slowdown in economic growth.

- A recession can be a good time to launch a business. FedEx, IBM, Disney, and Microsoft all started this way.

SAY WHAT?

GDP: Gross domestic product. This is the total value of all the goods and services produced or made in a country over a certain period of time (usually a year).

RISKY BUSINESS

There have been "economic bubbles" around many investments, including in Internet companies, housing, and even tulip bulbs! When the price of an investment rises more than people think it's worth, its value rapidly declines. The bubble bursts, leaving people with financial problems.

Depression
★ All-Time Low

THE BIG IDEA

A long-term decrease in economic activity; it sometimes spreads across several countries.

If you think Recession is all doom and gloom, wait until you hear my story. I'm Depression. I wait for a serious crisis — war, disease, stock market collapse — that kind of thing. Then I take hold and grip tight for at least a couple of years, a decade even.

I'm a real baddie. I push **unemployment rates** into double figures. I stop banks wanting to help companies start up or expand. People have less money to spend, so manufacturers stop making stuff. With me around the health of the population gets worse and people protest — often violently — because they are so unhappy. Boy, this is *not* a pretty picture.

- In the 3rd century CE the Roman Empire suffered a major depression caused by inflation, decreased trading, and political instability.

- During a recent economic recession in Greece (2009–2013), 50% of young people were unemployed.

SAY WHAT?

Unemployment rate: The percentage of the workforce (adults who are able to work) that does not have a job.

OLD TIMERS

The Great Depression was the most severe depression ever. It resulted from a massive crash in the New York Stock Exchange in 1929. The whole world suffered for at least 10 years. In most countries 25% of the population was unemployed.

Inflation
★ Price Riser

THE BIG IDEA

A rise in the general level of prices for goods and services.

Look at me, all puffed up and proud! I'm Inflation — a rise in the prices of goods and services. Economists measure me by figuring out a **consumer price index**. "How much is a loaf of bread?" they ask. "A first-class stamp?" "What did the plumber charge to fix that leak?" . . . and more. Comparing the answers to a list of the previous year's prices shows the rate at which I have changed.

Sure, if everything costs a little more year on year, it can be good, because I'm helping the economy grow. But if I make prices rise too quickly, and people's wages stay the same, they stop being able to buy things and that can only spell trouble.

- In Germany, in 1923, banknotes were worth so little that children used bundles of them as building blocks!

- The fastest rate of inflation ever was in Hungary in July 1946, when prices doubled every fifteen hours.

Globalization
⭐ The Great Connector

THE BIG IDEA

When different countries become better connected and reliant on each other through increased trading and interaction.

Hola! Namaste! Salut! Konnichiwa! Hello! A citizen of the world, I'm Globalization, a well-connected type whose high-tech comms enable trade across the globe.

I'm ancient really, but advances in transport and communications have seen my activity skyrocket in the last 50 years. Just imagine it taking months for headphones to arrive from China or for Pez candy to ship to Europe! Buying things made in places with lower wages means companies can sell them more cheaply back home. Better still, businesses that set up shop overseas make job opportunities for locals there that never existed before.

- The shipping container revolutionized globalization. These large steel boxes make it cheaper and easier to carry goods by sea, by rail, and on trucks.

- A true symbol of globalization, Coca-Cola operates in every country in the world except Cuba and North Korea.

⚡ SAY WHAT? ⚡

Multinational corporation: A large company, such as Apple or Amazon, that carries on business activities in at least two countries. Multinational corporations are a feature of globalization.

✳ RISKY BUSINESS ✳

Some say globalization allows wealthier countries to take advantage of poorer ones. Others say that it forces local companies out of business. And some think that **multinational corporations** have become too powerful, and tell governments what to do.

Loan

Short-Term Loan

Peer-to-Peer Lending

Mortgage

Credit Card

Debt

Bankruptcy

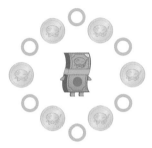

The Borrower Bunch

You won't always have enough money to buy
all the things you want or need. Luckily the members
of the Borrower Bunch are here to show you how to get
your hands on extra cash. Don't forget, though, you
will always need to pay it back (usually with interest!).
Friendly Loan kicks this show off, and you'll also meet
Short-Term Loan and Peer-to-Peer Lending. Mortgage
can help you buy a house and you can turn to Credit
Card for everyday purchases. Finally there are two
characters you'll run into if you don't pay back
what you borrow: Debt and Bankruptcy.
Watch out! They can be scary. . .

Loan

⭐ Cash Injector

THE BIG IDEA

A sum of money borrowed by a person or organization. It is repaid, with interest, at a later date.

Need a cash injection? Talk to me, Loan. Pretty much every business, company, and country in the world has needed my help at one time or another. Really, I'm the backbone of the economy!

Let's say you run a coffee shop. You need new equipment but don't have the cash to buy it. Have a chat with Bank and ask for me. You'll need to explain how I can help your business grow, and prove that you plan to pay me back. All the fine details are written in a **promissory note**. But take care. I almost always come hand-in-hand with Interest — remember your kindly money-lending aunt (*not*)?

- In ancient Rome people who did not repay loans sometimes became enslaved to their lenders.

- In 2018 the International Monetary Fund gave Argentina the biggest loan ever: $57 billion.

⚡ SAY WHAT? ⚡

Promissory note: A written promise to repay a loan. It states how much has been borrowed and the date by which it will be paid back, as well as the rate of interest.

✳ DO IT YOURSELF ✳

If you plan to go to college, you might need a student loan. This helps pay for tuition, books, and living costs, such as rent. Student loans often have lower interest rates than other types of loan. Repayments don't usually begin until the person graduates.

Short-Term Loan

★ Friend in Need

THE BIG IDEA

A sum of money borrowed from a financial organization. It is repaid, with interest, in under a year.

You've met useful Loan? A proper lifesaver, that one! But Loan has forms to fill out, contracts to read, and all this takes time. If time is something you don't have, you'll want me instead, Short-Term Loan.

As long as you have a job, I'm yours. A lender might not even check your **credit score**! I'm designed to meet immediate needs — repairing the storm-damaged roof of your coffee shop, say. But a word of caution, my friend. I come with high interest rates that increase over time and repayments must be speedy — usually by your next payday. Fail to pay and you might find yourself facing *bad* Debt.

- Short-term loans usually involve amounts under $1,000.

- In the United States there are 23,000 outlets of short-term loan companies — that's more than there are branches of McDonald's in the US.

⚡ SAY WHAT? ⚡

Credit score: A number showing how likely a person is to repay debts. It's based on such things as previous credit card spending and whether or not the person owns any property.

❋ THE SMALL PRINT ❋

Companies offering short-term loans often have very high interest rates. Let's say you borrow $100 at 10% interest, but have one week to pay it back. You will be paying $1.43 in interest every day (compared to about 3 cents a day if you had a year to pay back the same loan at the same rate).

Peer-to-Peer Lending
★ Crowd Funder

> **THE BIG IDEA**
>
> Also known as P2P lending. Instead of using a bank, people borrow money from other individuals via the Internet.

The baby of this Borrower Bunch, I'm the future of borrowing money. My name is **Peer-to-Peer** Lending, but you can call me P2P. Let me tell you how I work.

Operating online, companies that provide my services simply connect you with wannabe lenders. Say you have a proposal to develop a new drone. A lender who likes your proposal will offer up the cash. For the lender, Investment teams up with Interest to make healthy repayments. If your proposal appeals to several lenders, they might compete with each other by offering lower interest rates in order to secure a deal. Go get 'em!

- The first company to provide peer-to-peer lending was Zopa, which was launched in the UK in 2005.

- Some companies that arrange peer-to-peer lending spread loans out across lots of different borrowers, which decreases the risk.

> **SAY WHAT?**
>
> **Peer-to-peer**: Any system that features interactions between equals. It began as a way of sharing resources between different computers on a network.

> **✳ RISKY BUSINESS ✳**
>
> P2P is popular because it offers higher rates of interest than other forms of investment, such as savings accounts in banks. However, there is not a 100% guarantee that lenders will get their money back.

Mortgage
★ Home Loaner

THE BIG IDEA

A loan that individuals and businesses use to buy property. It is usually repaid, with interest, over a long-term period.

I'm Mortgage, the go-to borrower when you want to buy a piece of property (a house, office, shop, or land), but don't quite have the cash on hand.

Say you find your dream house with a den in the attic and a pool out back. It costs $250,000 but you only have $50,000 saved up. Don't panic! I can help you borrow $200,000 from Bank or some other financial organization. They'll ask loads of questions — about you, your income, the house — but if all goes well you'll get the cash. Expect Interest to jump on board (who else?!), but you'll have 30 years or so to pay it all back, month by month. Phew!

- In Scotland it's traditional to paint your front door red when you've repaid the mortgage.

- A "fixed-rate" mortgage has the same interest rate from beginning to end; with a "variable rate" the interest rate will go up and down.

SAY WHAT?

Repossession: This is when a borrower stops making payments and the lender forces them to sell whatever the loan was for — a house or car, say — in order to get back the money.

THE SMALL PRINT

Once you have taken out a mortgage, it is really important not to miss a payment. If you cannot keep up, you might face **repossession** and lose your house.

Credit Card

★ Flexible Friend

THE BIG IDEA

A form of payment where the organization that issues the card pays for something, and the cardholder pays them back.

Are you tired of flash Cash weighing your pockets down? Use me instead! I'm Credit Card, a handy rectangle of plastic used everywhere for buying things on **credit**. I'm just the ticket for online purchases, too.

I'm issued by Bank, or some other financial organization. When you use me to buy stuff, you're borrowing their money. You can pay it back bit by bit every month. Banks give rewards for responsible use, which could improve your credit score. But you should know that Interest adds to any amount left unpaid each month. And if you don't keep up with repayments . . . yep, Debt grows bigger and bigger!

- The first widely accepted credit card was issued by an American company called Diners Club in 1950.

- The highly exclusive, invitation-only Dubai First Royale MasterCard has gold trim, an embedded diamond, and no limit on credit.

SAY WHAT?

Credit: Money that you are allowed to borrow, and which the lender trusts that you will pay back in due course.

✳ MONEY HEROES ✳

Debit cards look like credit cards but they work differently. When someone uses a debit card, the money is taken out of their account rather than borrowed from the bank. It is harder to get into debt using a debit card, as you can usually only spend the money you have in the bank.

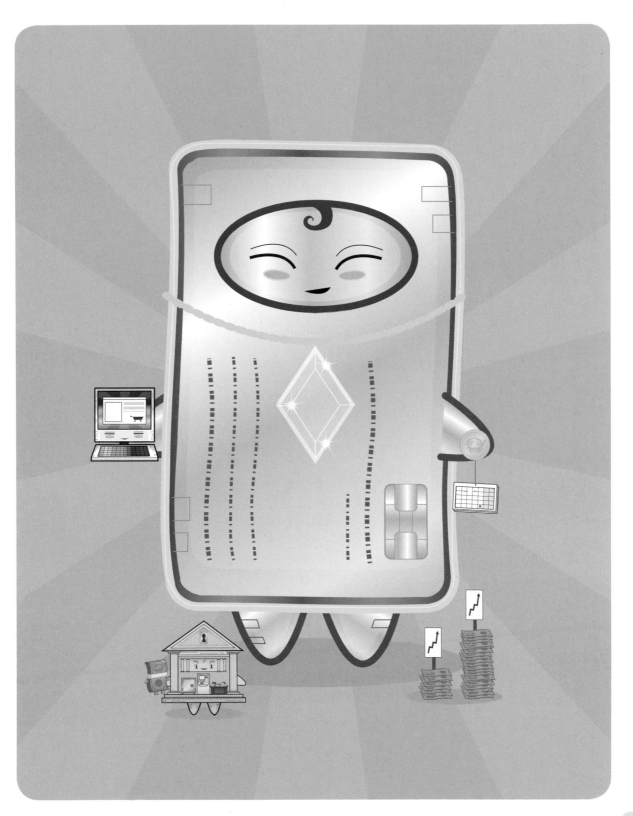

Debt

★ Two-Faced Score

THE BIG IDEA

Money that one person or organization has borrowed from another person or organization, agreeing to repay the sum later.

Use any member of the Borrower Bunch, and you'll be taking me on. I'm Debt. I can be good . . . but I can also be *bad*.

When you borrow money, you become a debtor. You have an **obligation** to repay the lender — your creditor. Know that I will be a part of your life until that happens. Spread payments over a long time and keep Interest low, and I'll help you borrow money safely: that's my good side. But fail to settle my score on time or according to the agreed terms and you will see my *bad* side. I will make you **default**, which could bring legal problems and future financial trouble. You don't want that, believe me.

- Many governments around the world have debts running into trillions.

- The biggest ever default by a business was by an American bank called Lehman Brothers; it went bankrupt in 2008, owing $613 billion in debts.

SAY WHAT?

Obligation: Something that you have to do, often because it is required by law.

Default: Failure to meet agreed conditions when paying back a loan.

✳ STRANGE BUT TRUE ✳

Countries often get into debt. That's because governments borrow money to pay for such things as roads, schools, and the military. Investors are usually happy to lend to governments because they're very likely to repay the loan.

Bankruptcy
★ Scary Declarer

THE BIG IDEA

A declaration made by a person or business who cannot pay back their debts and whose debts are then canceled.

Serious financial problems or a sudden crisis can bring **insolvency**. If there really are no other options, people turn to me: Bankruptcy. On declaring me, a debtor becomes legally bankrupt and their debts and bills are canceled. This gives them a chance for a fresh start. Yay-hey!

But wait, I have a nasty streak! You see, once I have been declared, I value the debtor's assets — house, car, possessions. And I sell them off to pay at least some of the money owed. *Then* I make sure that my Borrower Bunch pals are very unhelpful in future — not even ever-ready Credit Card will want to help. It's no party!

- In 2013 the US city of Detroit declared bankruptcy, owing over $18 billion.

- In the 1800s people who couldn't repay their debts were sent to special debtors' prisons; they had to stay there until the money was repaid.

⚡ **SAY WHAT?** ⚡

Insolvency: When a person or business cannot pay back their debts on time.

Filing a petition: The act of going to court with a request to start legal proceedings.

✳ **HOW IT WORKS** ✳

The process of declaring bankruptcy begins with **filing a petition** at a court of law. If a person or company decides to file a petition themselves, their bankruptcy is described as "voluntary." If a creditor files the petition, the bankruptcy is termed "involuntary."

Consumer Rights

Insurance

Pension

Identity Theft

Rainy-Day Fund

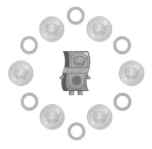

The Safety Set

Last but not least, here comes the Safety Set,
a bunch of helpful characters who'll keep you
and your money out of harm's way. Well, almost —
there's just one villainous individual lurking about
the place. . . But first, Consumer Rights will make sure
companies don't take advantage of you. Insurance will
have you covered if something bad or unexpected
happens. And when it comes to planning for the future,
Pension and Rainy-Day Fund are ready to step up to
the plate. So, the bad egg of the bunch? Why, that's
Identity Theft — worth getting to know just so
you can avoid a harmful encounter!

Consumer Rights

⭐ The Great Protector

THE BIG IDEA

A set of rules that businesses have to follow in order to protect people who buy their goods and services.

If you buy something that fails to meet expectations, call on me, Consumer Rights. I'm a superhero and I'll protect you against being treated unfairly when you spend your money. My regulations stop businesses carrying out **unfair practices**.

Say you buy a ticket to a theme park that advertises the scariest rollercoasters in the world, but when you arrive there are no rollercoasters! I'll help you get a refund on your ticket and maybe even **damages** for the time you've wasted. Messing with me can land a business in serious trouble. Its owners can end up in court and might face fines or even imprisonment.

- Delayed flights, faulty goods, injury, mis-selling, and poor train service are among the things you could make a claim against as a consumer.

- Aztec traders used a box divided into fixed sizes to measure things like corn accurately, so that people bought the exact amount they'd paid for.

SAY WHAT?

Unfair practice: Illegal activity that limits competition in business or misleads consumers.

Damages: Money paid in compensation in the case of financial loss or physical injury.

MONEY HEROES

Consumer organizations help protect people from being treated unfairly by businesses. They ask governments to make laws to stop unfair practices, and help people who want to complain about how they've been treated.

Insurance

★ Policy Maker

> **THE BIG IDEA**
>
> Protection that you buy in case something bad happens. Your insurance company gives you money to help you out.

Ever worry about losing your smartphone? Your pet getting sick? Falling off your bike and hurting yourself? Make friends with me and I can take your worries away. I'm Insurance, and I'm one smooth operator.

Take that smartphone of yours. Get it insured! Simply make a small, monthly payment (a premium) to an insurance company. Then, if your smartphone gets lost, damaged, or stolen, that company will pay for some (even all) of the cost of replacing it. Just check your **policy** for details! You can get insurance for all sorts of things: health care, lost property, accidents in the home — you name it.

- In 2008 a Dutch wine-maker insured his nose for $5 million, claiming his sense of smell was vital to his job.

- People have paid for insurance against some unusual things, such as alien abduction and being haunted by ghosts.

SAY WHAT?

Policy: A contract between an insurance company and the insured person. It sets out the details of what is being insured and for how much.

THE SMALL PRINT

You could end up paying a premium for many years. But if the event you have insured against (such as losing your smartphone) never happens, you won't get any of the money back. The insurance company keeps it.

Pension

★ Old Timer

THE BIG IDEA

A regular payment of money made to a person in his or her **retirement**.

Hi, I'm Pension. A safe pair of hands for your retirement, I'll help you save the money you need to live comfortably when you stop working. Here's how.

While you're employed, you pay a regular sum into a fund (that's me!). You can usually do this through your job, with the sum being a percentage of your income. Money Makers Investment and Interest team up to make me grow. Then, when you stop working, that fund (me) is all yours, paid in installments or as a **lump sum**. All you need to do is relax and enjoy a life of pottering in the garden and putting your feet up in a new pair of toasty slippers.

- In some countries, anyone who pays taxes also receives a pension from their government.

- One of the first-ever pensions was paid to soldiers by Roman Emperor Augustus in the 1st century BCE.

⚡ SAY WHAT? ⚡

Retirement: When a person stops working — usually at around the age of 66–67 years.

Lump sum: A single payment of money.

✳ MONEY HEROES ✳

An annuity is another financial product that helps you plan for your future. If you buy one it gives you a guaranteed regular payment until you die. The amount you pay for it is based on how long the company running the annuity thinks you will live for.

Identity Theft
⭐ Stolen Personality

THE BIG IDEA

When a criminal steals someone's personal details (date of birth, address), which they then use to pretend to be the other person.

So many characters in this book want to help you, but not me! I'm Identity Theft and I'm out to ruin your life. I'll steal private information about you and use it to commit **fraud**. I could take out a loan, start a credit card, or get a mortgage in your name. At the very least my activity will cost you time to put things right. At worst it will lose you money and damage your credit score. I'm mean, I tell you.

Want to stop me? Be VERY careful about sharing your personal data. Pay close attention to your bank account. And tear up private documents when you throw them out — I lurk in some unlikely places.

- In the 15th century Perkin Warbeck assumed the identity of a dead prince to make a claim to the English throne.

- From 2003 to 2008 New Yorker Thomas Parkin dressed up as his dead mother so he could cash her Social Security payments.

SAY WHAT?

Fraud: The crime of gaining money by deceiving or lying in some way. A person who does this is called a "fraudster."

✳ RISKY BUSINESS ✳

A lot of identity theft takes place online. To protect yourself on the Internet keep all of your passwords private and make sure they are not easily guessed. Don't click links from emails you don't recognize and only install apps and programs you trust.

Rainy-Day Fund
⭐ Back-Up Cash Stash

THE BIG IDEA

Money saved for unplanned expenses — for example, if your cat needs surgery on a broken paw.

Hi! I'm Rainy-Day Fund — your best friend when facing a pricey surprise. Say you have to replace a broken window after playing catch. I'll be right there to help you pay.

You see, I'm a little sum of money you keep separate from your **checking account** and only use in emergencies. Unlike Bond and Stock, I'm **liquid**, so I won't earn you interest. My great advantage is that you can get hold of me in a hurry! Choose me and you won't have to deal with Credit Card or Short-Term Loan. But please remember: once you use me, be sure to top me up again. Otherwise, I won't be there for next time, butter fingers!

- The country with the highest savings per household is tiny Luxembourg, in Europe.

- More than one-quarter of Americans have no money set aside to pay for sudden expenses.

SAY WHAT?

Checking account: A bank account into which you pay your salary and use for everyday spending and paying bills.

Liquid: Here, something that can easily be converted into cash.

MONEY HEROES

As an adult, a rainy-day fund can be a lifesaver if something really serious happens — say if you lose your job or become too sick to work. If you have enough to cover your daily expenses for three months, you can stay on top of your finances while you look for a new job or get better.

Glossary

Asset: A resource owned by a business or individual that they can sell to convert into money.

Blockchain: An online record of transactions that is stored across millions of computers.

Bullion: Precious metals (usually gold or silver) that are melted down and formed into bars or coins.

Checking account: A bank account into which you pay your salary and use for everyday spending.

Consumer: A person who buys or uses goods and services.

Consumer price index: The average prices of goods and services that every household needs.

Contract: A legal agreement that sets out the details of a business arrangement.

Counterfeit: To make a fake version of an item and try to pass it off as the real deal.

Coupon: A ticket that can be swapped for money off a product. It is also the annual interest payment made to someone who holds a bond.

Credit: Money that you are allowed to borrow, and which the lender trusts that you will pay back.

Creditor: An organization or individual that is owed money by another organization or individual.

Credit score: A number showing how likely a person is to repay debts.

Cryptocurrency: A digital currency that is not controlled by any government or bank.

Currency: The system of money that a country uses — for example, dollars ($) and euros (€).

Damages: Money paid in compensation in the case of financial loss or physical injury.

Debtor: An organization or individual that owes money to another organization or individual.

Default: Failure to meet agreed conditions when paying back a loan.

Deficit: When an organization spends more money than it takes in over a certain period, usually a year.

Deposit: An amount of cash placed in a bank account.

Dividend: A payment that a company makes to its shareholders.

Economy: The system of how money, goods, and services are made and used.

Employee: Any person who is paid wages when working for an organization.

Employer: An individual or organization that hires people to work for them, and pays them a wage.

Eurozone: 19 countries, all members of the European Union, that have the euro as their currency.

Exchange rate: How much one unit of a given currency will get you in another.

Expenditure: The spending of money by an individual or organization.

Fee: A fixed sum of money that is paid or charged for a service.

Filing a petition: The act of going to court with a request to start legal proceedings.

Finances: The money a person or company has at their disposal and the ways in which they use it.

Foodstuffs: Something that can be eaten as food, or used to make food.

Fraud: The crime of gaining money by deceiving or lying in some way.

GDP: Gross domestic product. The total value of all the goods and services produced or made in a country over a certain period of time.

Illegal: Something that an individual or organization is not allowed to do according to the law.

Income: Money earned on a regular basis, such as wages from a job or rent from a property.

Insolvency: When a person or business cannot pay back their debts on time.

Landfill: A big hole dug into the ground and used for storing waste.

Lender: An individual or organization (for example a bank) that lends money.

Liquid: Here, something that can easily be converted into cash.

Liquidate: To close down a company, often because it is failing. The company's owners must sell off any assets in order to pay their debts.

Lump sum: A single payment of money.

Market dominance: When just one organization controls most of the sale of a particular good or service in an area.

Multinational corporation: A large company, such as Apple or Amazon, that carries on business activities in at least two countries.

Obligation: Something that you have to do, often because it is required by law.

Peer-to-peer: Any system that features interactions between equals.

Percentage: A fraction of an amount based on hundredths of it. For example 10 percent is ten hundredths (10/100), which is 1/10.

Perpetual bond: A bond that has no maturity date. The organization that issues the bond pays interest forever.

Policy: A contract between an insurance company and the insured person. It sets out the details of what is being insured and for how much.

Pollution: Harmful substances that enter the natural environment.

Portfolio: The collection of different investments held by one company or individual.

Premium: The amount of money paid to a company for insuring something.

Principal: The amount of money lent to someone.

Profit: The money a business has left over once all of its costs have been paid (for example, on materials or staff).

Promissory note: A written promise to repay a loan. It states how much has been borrowed, date by which it will be paid back, and rate of interest.

Repossession: When a borrower stops making payments and a lender forces the sale of whatever the loan was for in order to get back the money.

Retailer: A seller of goods or services to customers (for example, a shopkeeper).

Retirement: When a person stops working — usually at around the age of 66–67 years.

Return: The profit earned on an investment.

Revenue: The income that an individual or organization gathers by selling goods or services.

Salary: The amount of money that is paid to someone when doing a regular job.

Share: One of the equal parts into which ownership of a company is divided.

Social security: A system governments use to provide money to ensure people have access to food and shelter.

Stock market: The people and organizations that buy and sell stocks.

Supply chain: The system of different people and businesses that take food, or other goods, from where they are produced to the customer.

Transaction: Any occasion on which goods or services are bought or sold.

Unfair practice: Illegal activity that limits competition in business or misleads consumers.

Utilities: Basic services such as water, electricity, gas, sewage, and Internet.

Wholesaler: A seller of manufactured goods or fresh produce to retailers.

Index